Eckert's
OUR FAVORITES
SPRING & SUMMER RECIPES
PEACH, BERRY, CORN, TOMATO & MORE

Special thanks to our talented friends…

The cover and interior images are courtesy of Joy McCullough.

The Basil Blackberry Hard Cider Cocktail
recipe on page 33 is courtesy of Liz Rotz.

Reedy Press

PO Box 5131

St. Louis, MO 63139, USA

www.reedypress.com

ISBN: 9781681065038

Design by Rich Roden

Printed in the United States of America

24 25 26 27 28 5 4 3 2 1

CONTENTS

INTRODUCTION

The Eckert family has been growing fruit for more than 100 years in rural Illinois, near St. Louis. Proud of their farming heritage and stewardship of the land, the Eckerts have cultivated and preserved their orchard business for eight generations.

Eckert's Orchards took root in 1837 after Johann Peter Eckert immigrated to Pittsburgh, Pennsylvania, from Dietzenbach in Hesse, Germany, and began farming. Johann's son Michael followed his father's instinctive love for the land and settled on a farm. We call that Drum Hill near Fayetteville, Illinois, which is 35 miles southeast of St. Louis. Fruit trees were planted on Michael's farm in 1862, and then Michael's son Henry followed suit. In 1890, Henry planted fruit trees on his Turkey Hill Farm in Belleville, Illinois. Henry's farm is now the hub of the Eckert's family business. This is where the family's largest orchard produces apples, peaches, strawberries, blackberries, and other fresh fruits and vegetables and where its Country Restaurant and Country Store operate year-round. Today the seventh and eighth generations of the Eckert family oversee the daily business operations.

This cookbook is a celebration of some of our favorite spring and summer recipes. You can start a meal with Judy's creamy tomato & cucumber salad or with some sweet strawberry bruschetta. Make a meal of pork tenderloin with balsamic peaches or farfalle with asparagus & mushrooms. And don't forget to take advantage of the spring and summer harvest with Grandma Ruth's peach cake or chocolate zucchini cake. We've even included some of our favorite cocktails including strawberry mojito remix and peachy sangria.

Come join us at Eckert's; choose some farm-fresh, spring and summer ingredients to make and enjoy your own Eckert's family favorites.

PEACHY SANGRIA

1 750-ml bottle of Eckert's Peach Wine

2 16-oz. cans of Eckert's Peach Hard Cider

16 oz. lemon lime soda

Fresh seasonal fruit

In a pitcher, combine ingredients. Serve immediately in glasses filled with ice and fresh seasonal fruit.

Eckert's

PEACH, PROSCUITTO & RICOTTA CROSTINI

- 12 slices Eckert's Bake at Home Bread or French baguette
- Olive oil
- 2-3 Tbs. fresh ricotta
- Freshly ground black pepper to taste
- 4 thin slices of prosciutto
- 1-2 Tbs. Eckert's Pure Honey
- 24 peach slices

Preheat oven to 400°F. Brush both sides of sliced bread with olive oil. Bake 4 to 6 minutes. Flip bread. Bake 4 to 6 minutes more. Remove from oven and cool. Spoon fresh ricotta onto each slice of toast and sprinkle with pepper. Tear the prosciutto into feathery pieces and drape a few slices over ricotta-covered toast. Drizzle each with honey and top with 2 peach slices. Makes 12 servings.

JUDY'S CREAMY TOMATO & CUCUMBER SALAD

- ¼ cup regular mayonnaise
- 2 Tbs. white vinegar
- 2 tsp. granulated sugar
- 2 homegrown tomatoes, cored and sliced
- 1 large homegrown cucumber, peeled and thinly sliced
- 1 medium sweet onion, thinly sliced (optional)
- Kosher salt to taste

In a small bowl, make dressing by whisking together first 3 ingredients; set aside. Place tomato slices on a platter or large plate, salt to taste. Top tomatoes with cucumbers and onions if using. Drizzle dressing on top and toss. Allow to rest and draw juices for 10 to 15 minutes. Serve immediately. Makes 3 to 4 servings.

TIP: Do not substitute light mayonnaise.

CHERRY TOMATO & FETA SALAD

- 4 cups (2 pints) grape or cherry tomatoes, halved
- ¾ cup diced red onion (2 small onions)
- ⅛ cup white balsamic vinegar
- 3 Tbs. olive oil
- ½ tsp. kosher salt
- ½ tsp. freshly ground black pepper
- ⅛ cup chopped, fresh basil leaves
- 4 oz. feta cheese, crumbled

Place tomato halves in a large bowl. Add onions, vinegar, olive oil, salt, pepper, and basil. Toss well, then gently fold feta into salad. Serve at room temperature. Makes 6 servings.

SUMMER ORZO SALAD WITH RED WINE VINAIGRETTE

RED WINE VINAIGRETTE

½ cup red wine vinegar

¼ cup fresh lemon juice

2-3 tsp. Eckert's Pure Honey

2 tsp. salt

¾ tsp. freshly ground black pepper

1 cup olive oil

ORZO SALAD

4 cups chicken broth

1½ cups uncooked orzo

1 (15-oz.) can garbanzo beans, drained and rinsed

1½ cups red cherry or grape tomatoes, halved

1 cup peeled and diced cucumbers

¾ cup finely chopped red onions

2 Tbs. chopped fresh basil leaves

2 Tbs. chopped fresh lemon thyme or lemon verbena

TO PREPARE VINAIGRETTE:

Mix vinegar, lemon juice, honey, salt, and pepper in a blender or shaker. Whisk in oil gradually. Season vinaigrette to taste with more salt and pepper if desired. Makes about 1¾ cups dressing. After dressing orzo salad, cover and refrigerate any remaining dressing for another salad.

TO PREPARE ORZO SALAD:

Pour broth into a large, heavy saucepan. Cover pan and bring broth to a boil over high heat. Stir in orzo. Cook until orzo is tender but still firm to the bite, stirring frequently, about 7 minutes. Drain orzo through a strainer. Transfer orzo to a large, wide bowl and toss until it cools slightly (can put in refrigerator to speed up the process). Toss orzo with beans, tomatoes, cucumbers, onion, and herbs. Add vinaigrette to orzo salad to your taste. Season salad with salt and pepper and serve at room temperature or chilled. Makes 5 to 6 servings.

SUMMER FRUIT & GREENS SALAD WITH POPPYSEED DRESSING

Blend all dressing ingredients. Place greens on a platter. Mix fruit and dressing together in a large bowl. Pour on top of greens and serve. Makes 6 servings.

DRESSING

3 Tbs. red wine vinegar

⅓ cup granulated sugar

1 tsp. dry mustard

¾ tsp. kosher salt

⅓ cup vegetable oil

1 Tbs. poppy seeds

SALAD

5-6 cups fresh salad greens

1½ cups cantaloupe, diced

1½ cups fresh blueberries

2 large peaches, peeled and sliced

4 medium beets, peeled and cut into ½-inch pieces

1 Tbs. olive oil

1 tsp. salt

Pepper to taste

4 scallions, chopped

2 tsp. lemon juice

⅓ cup crumbled feta

ROASTED BEETS WITH FETA CHEESE

Preheat oven to 450°F. Toss beets with olive oil, salt, and pepper on baking sheet. Roast in oven for about 35 minutes or until tender, turning beets once halfway through roasting. Transfer to bowl and toss with scallions and lemon juice. Top with crumbled feta. Makes 6 servings.

ECKERT'S PICK-YOUR-OWN SALAD

TO PREPARE DRESSING:

Combine all dressing ingredients in a heavy saucepan over medium heat. Stir constantly with whisk until dressing comes to a boil, about 3 to 4 minutes. Allow dressing to cool. Cover and refrigerate until serving.

TO PREPARE SALAD:

Combine all salad ingredients on a large platter or in a large salad bowl. Drizzle cold dressing on top. Toss gently. Makes 6 servings.

DRESSING

2 large eggs, beaten

½ cup apple cider vinegar

1 cup granulated sugar

1 tsp. salt

1 tsp. dry mustard

SALAD

8 cups red or green leaf lettuce, washed, dried, and torn into bite-size pieces

2 spring onions, thinly sliced

2 cups sliced strawberries, blueberries, and blackberries

½ cup sliced almonds, chopped pecans, or chopped walnuts

BLACKBERRY PEACH BOURBON SMASH SIPPER

¼ fresh peach, diced

4-6 blackberries

6 mint leaves

Ice

2 oz. bourbon

2 lime wedges

1 Tbs. simple syrup

2 oz. chilled ginger beer or sparkling water

Sugar

Sugar rim of the glass. Muddle 5 blackberries, diced peaches, and mint leaves in a cocktail shaker. Add ice, bourbon, lime juice from wedges, lime wedges, and simple syrup and shake well. Pour into a glass. Stir in ginger beer (or sparkling water) and garnish with a fresh blackberry, peach slices, mint leaves, and lime.

ANGIE'S CORN SAUTÉ

Cut kernels off of corn cobs. Using the back of a knife, press hard on the empty ears of corn to extract the "milky" substance from cobs. Melt butter in a large skillet. Add onions and sauté for 2 to 4 minutes, until soft. Add corn, milky substance, and water. Sauté for 8 minutes over medium-low heat. Season to taste with salt and pepper. Then add cream and continue to cook about 2 minutes or until cream is warm. Makes 10 to 12 servings.

- 6 cups fresh corn, cut from the cob (12 ears)
- 4 Tbs. butter
- ¼-½ cup diced sweet onion
- 2 Tbs. water
- Salt and white pepper to taste
- 4 Tbs. heavy cream

CORN O'BRIEN

Melt butter in a large skillet. Add corn, peppers, and onions with 1 cup of water. Bring to a low boil. Stir frequently for 5 minutes.

Serve immediately or pour corn mixture onto a rimmed sheet pan to cool. Once cooled, freeze mixture in plastic quart freezer bags.

TIP: To defrost corn: Place mixture in a microwave-safe container. Microwave on medium heat for 6 to 8 minutes or until hot. Makes 4 to 6 servings.

4 Tbs. butter

5 cups fresh corn, cut from cob (about 10 ears)

½ cup red bell pepper, diced

½ cup green bell pepper, diced

½ cup sweet onions, diced

1 cup water

Salt and pepper to taste

SUMMER FRUIT SALSA & CINNAMON CRISPS

- 3 cups fresh strawberries, with stems removed and berries chopped
- 1 large banana, peeled and chopped
- 1 medium peach, unpeeled and chopped
- 2 kiwi fruits, peeled and chopped
- 3 Tbs. lime juice
- 4 tsp. Eckert's Pure Honey
- ½ tsp. ground cinnamon
- ¼ tsp. ground nutmeg

Stir together first 4 ingredients in a big bowl. Mix lime juice and honey and drizzle over fruit; stir gently to coat. Sprinkle cinnamon and nutmeg over fruit; stir gently. Cover with plastic wrap and chill fruit salsa in the refrigerator at least 30 minutes. Serve fruit salsa with Cinnamon Crisps. Makes 2⅔ cups fruit salsa.

CINNAMON CRISPS

4 (8-inch) flour tortillas

Vegetable cooking spray

2 Tbs. sugar

¾ tsp. ground cinnamon

Preheat oven to 350°F. Spray one side of each tortilla with vegetable cooking spray. Stir together sugar and cinnamon in small bowl. Sprinkle sugar mixture over each tortilla. Cut tortillas into 8 wedges with pizza cutter. Place about 1 inch apart on an ungreased baking sheet. Bake at 350°F for 12-15 minutes or until lightly brown. Cool. Makes 32 cinnamon crisps.

BLACKBERRY MOJITO

2 oz. rum

½ oz. freshly squeezed lime juice

6 mint leaves

¾ oz. simple syrup

2 oz. club soda

1 cup of ice

Blackberries and mint to garnish

Muddle blackberries, mint, lime juice, and simple syrup in a cocktail shaker. Add a cup of ice and rum. Shake well. Pour everything into a cocktail glass. Top with club soda and stir. Garnish with lime slice and blackberries.

MARINATED KABOBS

Whisk all marinade ingredients in a small bowl. Mix marinade and chicken, pork, or beef in a gallon-size zipper-lock plastic bag; seal bag and refrigerate, turning once or twice, until meat has marinated for at least 30 minutes, up to 2 hours. Preheat grill to medium-low. Meanwhile, lightly coat vegetables by tossing in medium bowl with oil, salt and pepper to taste. Remove meat pieces from bag; discard marinade. Thread meat and vegetables alternately onto skewers. Grill, turning each kabob one quarter turn every 2 minutes, until meat and vegetables are lightly browned and meat is fully cooked, about 8 to 10 minutes. Check for doneness by cutting into one of the meat pieces. Remove kabobs from grill. Serve immediately. Makes 8 kabobs (4 servings).

MARINADE

½ to ¾ cup olive oil

6 small garlic cloves, peeled and minced (about 2 Tbs.)

¼ cup minced fresh cilantro or minced mint leaves

1-2 tsp mixed dried Italian herbs

Salt and pepper to taste

MEAT

1½ lbs. boneless, skinless chicken breasts or thighs, pork, or beef, cut into 1 to 1½-inch pieces

VEGETABLES

3 cups of mixed vegetables (½-inch zucchini rounds; chunks of red or green bell pepper; onion wedges; whole medium mushrooms; large peeled garlic cloves)

2 to 3 Tbs. olive oil to coat vegetables

Kosher salt and freshly cracked black pepper

8 bamboo skewers, soaked in water

FAMILY FAVORITE GRILL BUNDLES

- 1 tsp. onion salt
- ¼ tsp. pepper
- ½ tsp. granulated garlic
- 1 lb. ground beef, browned
- ½ cup potatoes, unpeeled, uncooked, cut into ¼-inch cubes
- ½ cup fresh corn, uncooked, cut from the cob (1 ear)
- ½ cup carrots, cut into ½-inch pieces
- ½ cup fresh green beans, trimmed
- ½ cup shredded cheddar cheese, (optional)
- 8 (9-inch) squares heavy-duty foil

Preheat grill or oven to 375°F. Create a seasoning mix by combining onion salt, pepper, and garlic. Set aside. Combine ground beef, potatoes, corn, carrots, and green beans with 1 teaspoon of the seasoning mix. Spoon equal portions onto the center of each foil square. Seal. Grill 35 to 40 minutes. If desired, open bundle after cooking and add cheese. Reseal to allow cheese to melt. Makes 8 servings.

PEACH PORK CHOPS

- 1 Tbs. vegetable oil
- 4 boneless pork chops, 1-inch thick
- ¾ tsp. salt, divided
- ½ tsp. pepper, divided
- ½ cup chicken broth
- ½ cup Eckert's Peach Preserves
- 2 cups peeled, sliced peaches
- ¼ tsp. ground ginger
- 1 Tbs. Eckert's Honey Mustard
- 1 Tbs. apple cider vinegar

Heat oil in a large stainless steel sauté pan over medium-high heat. Season the pork chops with ½ teaspoon salt and ¼ teaspoon pepper. Place the pork chops in a single layer in the pan and brown for 2 minutes per side. Remove the pork chops from the pan and set aside. Add the broth and cook over high heat, scraping up browned bits from the pan. Reduce the heat to low.

Place peach preserves, peaches, ginger, honey mustard, vinegar, remaining ¼ teaspoon salt, and ¼ teaspoon pepper in the pan and stir to combine. Return the pork to the pan and baste with the peach mixture. Cover the pan and simmer for 15 minutes or until the internal temperature of the pork reaches 145°F. Makes 4 servings.

PORK TENDERLOIN WITH BALSAMIC PEACHES

1 pork tenderloin (about 1 lb.), silver skin removed

3-4 fresh rosemary sprigs, rinsed and blotted dry

Black pepper and salt to taste

2 Tbs. butter, divided

2 fresh peaches, peeled and sliced

2 Tbs. aged balsamic (white or dark) vinegar

1 Tbs. olive oil

Place pork tenderloin on a sheet of plastic wrap or butcher paper. Lay rosemary stems on pork and season with pepper. Wrap pork in plastic wrap or butcher paper and place in refrigerator for 1 to 2 hours. Preheat oven to 375°F. Remove pork from refrigerator and allow it to come to room temperature, about 30 to 40 minutes. Remove rosemary stems and dispose. Salt pork. Add 1 tablespoon butter and 1 tablespoon olive oil to a large stainless steel skillet on high heat. Brown each side of tenderloin for 2 to 3 minutes. Remove pork and place in an oven-safe dish. Bake pork until it reaches an internal temperature of 145°F (approximately 20 minutes).

Meanwhile, over medium heat, add remaining tablespoon of butter to the stainless steel skillet. Place peaches in the skillet. Sauté peaches for 2 minutes per side for a total of 4 minutes. Turn heat to low and add 2 tablespoons balsamic vinegar. Let the sauce reduce by ⅔, about 3 to 4 minutes. Place peaches and sauce in a small bowl. Serve pork and warm peaches together. Makes about 4 servings.

PEACHY MULE

5-6 peach slices

1½ oz. peach vodka

1 cup ice

4-5 oz. ginger beer

In a copper mug, muddle 2-3 slices of fresh peaches. Add vodka and top with ice. Stir well before topping with ginger beer. Garnish with remaining peach slices.

- 4-6 tomatoes, diced
- 5 Tbs. extra virgin olive oil
- 2 tsp. fresh lemon juice
- ⅓ cup chopped, fresh basil
- Salt and pepper to taste
- 1 lb. spaghetti or fettuccine pasta
- ½ cup freshly grated Parmesan cheese

FRESH TOMATO PASTA

Mix together tomatoes, oil, lemon juice, basil, and salt and pepper; set aside. Bring large pot of salted water to a boil and add pasta, cook until al dente according to package directions. Drain pasta and immediately toss with tomato mixture; sprinkle with cheese and serve at once. Makes 4 to 6 servings.

FARFALLE WITH ASPARAGUS & MUSHROOMS

- 1 lb. farfalle pasta
- 1 cup reserved hot pasta water
- 3 Tbs. unsalted butter
- 1 lb. cremini mushrooms or morel mushrooms, trimmed and thickly sliced
- 1 lb. thin asparagus, trimmed and cut crosswise into 1-inch pieces
- 1 cup mascarpone cheese
- Pinch of freshly grated nutmeg
- ¾ cup toasted walnuts, coarsely chopped, divided
- ¼ to ½ cup freshly grated Parmesan cheese
- Salt and pepper to taste

Bring a large pot of salted water to boil. Add the farfalle and cook until al dente according to package instructions. Stir often to prevent the pasta from sticking together. Drain, reserving 1 cup of the hot pasta liquid. Meanwhile, melt the butter in a large, heavy skillet over medium heat. Add the mushrooms and sauté until they are tender and most of their juices have evaporated, about 5 minutes. Add the asparagus and sauté until it is crisp-tender, about 5 minutes. Stir in the mascarpone and nutmeg. Add the cooked farfalle and toss until the cheese coats the pasta, adding the reserved cooking liquid ¼ cup at a time to moisten. Stir in ½ cup of the walnuts. Season the pasta to taste with salt and pepper. Mound the pasta in a large, wide serving bowl. Sprinkle with the Parmesan cheese and remaining ¼ cup of walnuts and serve. Makes 4 servings.

THREE-CHEESE BLACKBERRY QUESADILLAS WITH PEACH SALSA

Stir together goat cheese, cream cheese, and Parmesan cheese until blended. Add grated carrots; mix well. Spread cheese mixture equally on half of each tortilla; top with drained blackberries. Fold over. Toast tortillas, in batches, in a lightly greased, large nonstick skillet or griddle over medium-high heat, 1 to 2 minutes on each side or until golden brown. Cut into 3 wedges, and serve with Peach Salsa. Makes 8 servings.

TIP: Cheese/carrot filling can be made 2 to 3 days ahead of time. Cover and refrigerate. Remove from refrigerator about 1 hour before using so that it is easier to spread.

- 4 oz. goat cheese, softened
- 1 pkg (8 oz.) cream cheese, softened
- ½ cup freshly grated Parmesan
- ½ cup peeled carrots, grated (optional)
- 8 (6-inch) soft flour tortillas
- 1⅔ cups fresh or frozen (defrosted) blackberries; well drained, cut in half
- Peach Salsa, about 1 cup

PEACH SALSA

- 4 cups peaches, unpeeled and diced
- ½ cup red onion, small dice
- ½ cup green bell pepper, small dice
- ½ cup red bell pepper, small dice
- 2-3 Tbs. Eckert's Pure Honey

Place ingredients in a medium bowl. Mix all ingredients together. Adjust seasonings to taste. Cover and chill. For best flavor, allow salsa to come to room temperature about 1 hour before serving.

TIP: Add a little more heat to this recipe by including 1 teaspoon fresh chopped cilantro and 2 teaspoons of finely chopped fresh jalapeño pepper.

STRAWBERRY, GRILLED TURKEY & GOAT CHEESE PANINI

Cut goat cheese log into 4 equal portions. Spread on 4 bread slices. Top with turkey, basil leaves, and strawberries. Spread 1½ teaspoons pepper jelly on one side of remaining bread slices; place bread slices, jelly side down, on top of goat cheese. Brush sandwiches with melted butter. Grill in pan 2 minutes per side. Garnish. Makes 4 servings.

- 1 (4 oz.) goat cheese log, softened
- 8 Italian bread slices
- 8 oz. thinly sliced smoked turkey
- 8 fresh basil leaves
- ½ to ¾ cup sliced fresh strawberries
- 2 Tbs. Eckert's Red Pepper Jelly
- 2 Tbs. butter, melted
- 4 strawberry halves, for garnish

STRAWBERRY MOJITO REMIX

- 1½ oz. vodka
- 1 oz. simple syrup
- 1 oz. fresh lime juice
- ½ cup fresh strawberries, sliced
- 6 mint leaves
- Ice
- 3 oz. Eckert's Well Red Strawberry Hard Cider or Eckert's Strawberry Wine

In a cocktail glass, muddle simple syrup, lime juice, strawberries, and mint. Add vodka, ice, and hard cider or wine. Stir well. Garnish with strawberries and mint.

- 2 medium tomatoes, cored and sliced
- ½-1 tsp. kosher salt
- ½ red onion, thinly sliced
- 1 tsp. to ½ Tbs. granulated sugar
- 2 medium peaches, peeled, sliced from pit
- 2-4 Tbs. olive oil
- 1-2 Tbs. apple cider vinegar
- 8 oz. fresh mozzarella cheese, sliced
- Basil leaves (optional)

PEACH TOMATO MOTZ

On a platter, alternate salted slices of tomato with thin slices of red onion. Sprikle with sugar. Continue to alternate with peach slices. Drizzle with olive oil and apple cider vinegar. Lastly, tuck in mozzarella slices. Makes 4 to 6 servings.

SCRATCH PIE DOUGH

2½ cups all-purpose flour

1½ tsp salt

1 cup of cold butter or cold vegetable shortening, cut into ½-inch cubes

6-10 Tbs. ice cold water

Extra flour for dough preparation

In a large bowl, whisk flour and salt. Using a pastry cutter or 2 forks to incorporate, add butter or shortening cubes to flour mixture in batches. When all butter or shortening is incorporated and the mixture resembles coarse crumbs, stir in 1 tablespoon of cold water at a time, adding just enough to allow the dough to form a ball. The dough will be sticky but not wet. If it cannot be formed into a ball, add more water. Divide dough into 2 equal portions, pat into 2 disks about 1 inch thick. Wrap disks in plastic wrap. Chill for at least 1 hour or up to 2 days.

Once dough is cooled, lightly flour a work surface and a rolling pin. Starting in the center of the disk, roll the dough into a 12-inch circle about ⅛-inch thick. Transfer the dough to a pie pan using a stainless steel spatula if needed. Trim pie dough with a knife to fit the pie pan. Proceed with pie per your recipe instructions.

Makes 2 pie crusts.

TIP: If using lard instead of butter or shortening, increase flour to 3 cups and use 1 cup plus 2 tablespoons of pure lard. Follow above recipe as directed.

SWEET STRAWBERRY BRUSCHETTA

Toast bread. Heat medium skillet over high heat. Add brown sugar, lemon zest, and juice; cook, stirring constantly until sugar melts and mixture begins to bubble, about 1 to 2 minutes. Add strawberries and stir until juices begin to release and berries are just starting to heat, about 30 seconds. Remove immediately from heat. Spread 1 tablespoon of goat cheese on each piece of toast. Top with warm berries. Drizzle with honey. Makes 4 servings.

- 4 slices French bread, cut into ½- to ¾-inch thickness
- 6 Tbs. light brown sugar
- 1 tsp. grated lemon zest
- 2 tsp. freshly squeezed lemon juice
- 3 cups strawberries, hulled and diced
- 4 Tbs. goat cheese, at room temperature
- 4 Tbs. of Eckert's Pure Honey

1⅓ cups granulated sugar

⅓ cup all-purpose flour

2 cups strawberries, hulled and sliced

2 cups rhubarb, chopped into 1-inch pieces

1 unbaked Eckert's Frozen 9-Inch Pie Crust (*or see page 27 for recipe*)

2 Tbs. butter, cut into pieces

CRUMB TOPPING

1 cup all-purpose flour

⅓ cup granulated sugar

½ tsp. cinnamon

¼ tsp. salt

½ cup cold butter, cut into pieces

GLAZE

1 tsp. water

2 Tbs. powdered sugar, sifted

STRAWBERRY RHUBARB CRUMB TOP PIE

Preheat oven to 375°F. In a medium bowl, combine granulated sugar and flour and set aside. In a large mixing bowl combine strawberries and rhubarb; add sugar/flour mixture to fruit. Pour contents into pie shell and dot with butter. To prepare crumb topping: in a medium bowl combine flour, granulated sugar, cinnamon, and salt. Cut butter into mixture until topping is crumbly. Sprinkle topping over top of fruit. Bake for 20 minutes: reduce temperature to 350°F and continue to bake until rhubarb is tender when tested with a toothpick or the point of a paring knife. To prepare glaze: combine water with powdered sugar and mix well; drizzle glaze over top of pie. Makes 6 to 8 servings.

RUTH'S GLAZED STRAWBERRY PIE

Using a potato masher, crush 2 cups of berries in a saucepan. Add granulated sugar and cornstarch to crushed berries. Cook and stir 4 to 5 minutes over medium heat until thick and clear. Add lemon juice. Cool. Cut remaining berries in halves and add to cooled mixture. Pour into baked pie shell and chill at least 2 hours. Top with whipped cream and serve. Makes 6 to 8 servings.

- 2 quarts (8 cups) strawberries, hulled and divided
- 1 cup granulated sugar
- 4 Tbs. cornstarch
- 1 tsp. lemon juice
- 1 pre-baked Eckert's Frozen 9-Inch Pie Crust (*or see page 27 for recipe*)
- Whipped cream for garnish

- 1 unbaked Eckert's Frozen 9-Inch Pie Crust (*or see page 27 for recipe*)
- 1 cup rhubarb, thinly sliced in ½-inch pieces
- 3 medium eggs, slightly beaten
- ¼ cup brown sugar
- ¾ cup granulated sugar
- 1 cup whole milk
- 1 tsp. pure vanilla extract
- Dash of cinnamon
- Dash of nutmeg

NOTE: You may have extra custard filling.

ECKERT'S RHUBARB CUSTARD PIE

Preheat oven to 400°F. Partially bake pie crust for 6 to 8 minutes.

While crust is baking, whisk eggs, sugars, milk, vanilla, cinnamon, and nutmeg together in a medium bowl.

Remove crust from oven. Reduce oven temperature to 375°F. Place rhubarb pieces in partially baked pie crust. Pour egg mixture over the rhubarb. Bake for 35 minutes or until custard is just set on top. Allow pie to rest for 10 to 15 minutes before cutting. Cool fully, cover, and refrigerate if not serving immediately. Makes 6 to 8 servings.

BLACKBERRY PEACH CRISP

- 2 cups blackberries
- 2 lbs (6 cups) peeled and sliced ripe peaches
- ½ cup granulated sugar
- 2 tsp. fresh lemon juice
- 1 cup quick-cooking oats
- ¾ cup all-purpose flour
- ¾ cup light brown sugar
- ½ tsp. salt
- ½ tsp. ground cinnamon
- ⅛ tsp. ground nutmeg
- 1 stick plus 1 Tbs. cold, unsalted butter, cubed

Preheat the oven to 375°F. In a large bowl, gently toss the blackberries, peaches, granulated sugar, and lemon juice. Pour into an 8 × 11 glass baking dish.

In a medium bowl, toss the oats with the flour, brown sugar, salt, cinnamon, and nutmeg. Using your fingers, mix in the butter until the topping is crumbly. Sprinkle topping over the fruit and bake for 50 to 60 minutes or until the topping is golden brown. Rest 30 minutes before serving. Makes 8 servings.

BASIL BLACKBERRY HARD CIDER COCKTAIL

- 3-4 fresh blackberries
- 1 oz. fresh lemon juice
- 1 oz. gin
- 2-3 basil leaves
- Ice
- 5 oz. Eckert's Berried Alive Blackberry Hard Cider

Muddle blackberries in a cocktail shaker. Add lemon juice, gin, and basil leaves to shaker. Shake it well. Strain the cocktail shaker into a glass with clean ice. Top with hard cider. Garnish with additional blackberries and basil if desired.

BLACKBERRY & PEACH COMPOTE

3 Tbs. Eckert's Pure Honey

¾ tsp. finely grated lime peel

1 tsp. fresh lime juice

Pinch of salt

3 firm, ripe peaches, halved

1 cup fresh blueberries or blackberries, cleaned

In a small, ½-quart saucepan combine honey, grated lime, lime juice, and salt. Cook over medium heat, stirring frequently, until well-combined and smooth, about 1 minute. Let cool slightly. Cut each peach half into wedges ¼- to ½-inch thick and cut crosswise into halves or thirds. Put peaches and berries in a bowl and drizzle the warm honey mixture over top; toss gently. Serve in individual glass bowls or martini glasses. Makes 6 servings.

PEACH SMASH COCKTAIL

1 ripe peach, sliced

2 oz. peach vodka

4 oz. lemonade

1 oz. simple syrup

1 oz. bourbon

½ cup ice

In a cocktail shaker, muddle half of the peaches. Add remaining ingredients. Shake well. Strain into glass with ice. Garnish with remaining peach slices.

- 2 cups all-purpose flour, sifted
- 1 Tbs. baking powder
- ¼ tsp. baking soda
- ⅛ tsp. ground allspice
- ⅓ cup packed brown sugar
- ⅓ cup melted butter
- 1 large egg, beaten
- 1 cup sour cream
- 3 Tbs. milk
- ⅔ cup peaches, peeled and chopped

CAROLE'S PEACHY MUFFINS

Preheat oven to 400°F. In a large bowl, combine flour, baking powder, baking soda, allspice, and brown sugar; set aside. In another small bowl, stir butter and egg into milk and sour cream. Add to flour mixture, stirring just enough to moisten. Add peaches and stir until just mixed (batter will be lumpy). Fill greased, regular-sized muffin tins ⅔ full (don't use paper liners). Bake for 25 minutes or until golden brown. Cool for 2 to 5 minutes. Remove muffins from tin and allow to fully cool. Makes 12 servings.

GRANDMA RUTH'S PEACH CAKE

- 1 Tbs. butter, softened
- 2-3 peaches, peeled and sliced
- 1 cup granulated sugar, divided
- 2 large eggs
- ½ cup all-purpose flour
- 1 tsp. baking powder
- ½ cup boiling water
- Whipped cream for garnish

Preheat oven to 350°F. Butter an 8 × 8 glass baking dish. Put sliced peaches in prepared baking pan and sprinkle peaches with ¼ cup sugar. In mixing bowl with electric mixer, beat eggs until very light, about 6 to 8 minutes; add remaining sugar 1 tablespoon at a time, beating after each addition. Stir in flour and baking powder. Gradually add water and mix well. Pour batter over peaches. Bake for 35 minutes; do not remove from pan while cooling. May be served warm or cool. When ready to serve, cut into 6 pieces. Top with whipped cream and garnish with a peach slice. Makes 6 servings. This recipe can be doubled and put into a 9 × 13 glass pan.

ECKERT'S BUTTERCREAM FROSTING

¾ cup strawberries, sliced

¾ cup butter, softened

1 (32 oz.) package powdered sugar

Process strawberries in blender or food processor until puréed (purée should measure about ½ cup). Beat butter at medium speed with electric mixer until creamy; gradually add powdered sugar alternately with puréed strawberries, beating until well blended after addition of strawberries. Makes 5 to 6 cups.

TIP: For peach buttercream, substitute ¾ cup peeled and sliced peaches.

JUANITA'S SPEEDY SPONGE CAKE

Preheat oven to 350°F. In a small bowl, beat eggs until light and thick, 5 to 6 minutes. Slowly add granulated sugar and continue beating for 2½ minutes. Fold in flour, baking powder, and salt all at once. Add milk, butter, and vanilla and mix well. Pour into a greased and floured 8 × 8 baking pan. Bake for 30 minutes or until top is golden brown. Makes 9 servings.

TIP: The secret to perfect texture in this recipe is beating the eggs for 5 to 6 minutes.

- 2 large eggs
- 1 cup granulated sugar
- 1 cup all-purpose flour
- 1 tsp. baking powder
- ⅛ tsp. salt
- ½ cup hot milk, not boiling
- 1 Tbs. butter, melted
- 1 tsp. vanilla extract

CHOCOLATE ZUCCHINI CAKE

- ½ cup butter, softened
- ⅓ cup vegetable oil
- 1¾ cups granulated sugar
- 2 large eggs
- 1 tsp. vanilla extract
- ½ cup sour milk*
- 2¼ cups all-purpose flour
- 4 Tbs. cocoa powder
- ½ tsp. baking powder
- 1 tsp. baking soda
- 2 cups grated zucchini, unpeeled
- ⅔ cup chocolate chips, divided
- Non-stick vegetable cooking spray

Preheat oven to 325°F. With electric mixer, cream butter, oil, and sugar. Add eggs, vanilla, and sour milk. Mix thoroughly.

Blend in dry ingredients. Stir in zucchini and ¼ cup chocolate chips. Pour batter into a 9 × 13 baking pan coated with cooking spray. Using remaining chocolate chips, sprinkle evenly on top of batter. Bake 40 to 45 minutes. Makes 12 servings.

TIP: The batter can be put into paper-lined muffin cups and baked 22 minutes.

***TO PREPARE SOUR MILK:**

Add ½ tablespoon of vinegar to milk to total ½ cup. Let sit 5 minutes.